Prayer Journal

This book belongs to

_____

Date: / /

Today's Verse

_____

_____

_____

_____

Date: / /

Today I am Grateful For...

- _____

- _____

- _____

- _____

Date: / /

Lord teach me to...

_____

_____

_____

_____

"Give thanks in all circumstances; for this is God's will
for you in Christ Jesus." Thessalonians 5:18

Date: /   /

Today's Verse

_____
_____
_____
_____

Date: /   /

Today I am Grateful For...

_____
_____
_____
_____

Date: /   /

Lord teach me to...

_____
_____
_____
_____

"The righteous person may have many troubles,
but the Lord delivers him from them all." Psalm 34:19

Date: / /

Today's Verse

_____
_____
_____
_____
_____

Date: / /

Today I am Grateful For...

_____
_____
_____
_____

Date: / /

Lord teach me to...

_____
_____
_____
_____

The Lord will fight for you; you need only to be still."
Exodus 14:14

Date: /   /

Today's Verse

_____
_____
_____
_____

Date: /   /

Today I am Grateful For...

_____
_____
_____
_____

Date: /   /

Lord Teach me To...

_____
_____
_____
_____

"For I am the Lord your God who takes hold of your
right hand and says to you, Do not fear; I will help you."
Isaiah 41:13

Date: /   /

Today's Verse

_____
_____
_____
_____

Date: /   /

Today I am Grateful For...

_____
_____
_____
_____

Date: /   /

Lord teach me to...

_____
_____
_____
_____

"The Lord is near to all who call on Him." Psalm 145:18

Date: / /

Today's Verse

_____

_____

_____

_____

Date: / /

Today I am Grateful For...

- _____

- _____

- _____

- _____

Date: / /

Lord teach me to...

_____

_____

_____

_____

"Give thanks in all circumstances; for this is God's will
for you in Christ Jesus." Thessalonians 5:18

Date: /   /

Today's Verse

_____
_____
_____
_____

Date: /   /

Today I am Grateful For...

_____
_____
_____
_____

Date: /   /

Lord teach me to...

_____
_____
_____
_____

"The righteous person may have many troubles,
but the Lord delivers him from them all." Psalm 34:19

Date: / /

Today's Verse

_____
_____
_____
_____

Date: / /

Today I am Grateful For...

_____
_____
_____
_____

Date: / /

Lord teach me to...

_____
_____
_____
_____

The Lord will fight for you; you need only to be still."
Exodus 14:14

Date: /   /

Today's Verse

_____
_____
_____
_____

Date: /   /

Today I am Grateful For...

_____
_____
_____
_____

Date: /   /

Lord Teach me To...

_____
_____
_____
_____

"For I am the Lord your God who takes hold of your
right hand and says to you, Do not fear; I will help you."
Isaiah 41:13

Date: / /

Today's Verse

_____
_____
_____
_____

Date: / /

Today I am Grateful For...

_____
_____
_____
_____

Date: / /

Lord teach me to...

_____
_____
_____
_____

"The Lord is near to all who call on Him." Psalm 145:18

Date: /   /

Today's Verse

_____
_____
_____
_____

Date: /   /

Today I am Grateful For...

- _____
- _____
- _____
- _____

Date: /   /

Lord teach me to...

_____
_____
_____
_____

"Give thanks in all circumstances; for this is God's will
for you in Christ Jesus." Thessalonians 5:18

Date: / /

Today's Verse

_____
_____
_____
_____

Date: / /

Today I am Grateful For...

_____
_____
_____
_____

Date: / /

Lord teach me to...

_____
_____
_____
_____

"The righteous person may have many troubles,
but the Lord delivers him from them all." Psalm 34:19

Date: /   /

Today's Verse

_____
_____
_____
_____
_____

Date: /   /

Today I am Grateful For...

_____
_____
_____
_____
_____

Date: /   /

Lord teach me to...

_____
_____
_____
_____
_____

The Lord will fight for you; you need only to be still."
Exodus 14:14

Date: / /

Today's Verse

_____

_____

_____

_____

Date: / /

Today I am Grateful For...

_____

_____

_____

_____

Date: / /

Lord Teach me To...

_____

_____

_____

_____

"For I am the Lord your God who takes hold of your
right hand and says to you, Do not fear; I will help you."
Isaiah 41:13

Date: / /

Today's Verse

_____
_____
_____
_____
_____

Date: / /

Today I am Grateful For...

_____
_____
_____
_____

Date: / /

Lord teach me to...

_____
_____
_____
_____

"The Lord is near to all who call on Him." Psalm 145:18

Date: / /

Today's Verse

_____
_____
_____
_____

Date: / /

Today I am Grateful For...

• _____
• _____
• _____
• _____

Date: / /

Lord teach me to...

_____
_____
_____
_____

"Give thanks in all circumstances; for this is God's will
for you in Christ Jesus." Thessalonians 5:18

Date: / /

Today's Verse

_____
_____
_____
_____

Date: / /

Today I am Grateful For...

_____
_____
_____
_____

Date: / /

Lord teach me to...

_____
_____
_____
_____

"The righteous person may have many troubles,
but the Lord delivers him from them all." Psalm 34:19

Date: /   /

Today's Verse

_____
_____
_____
_____
_____

Date: /   /

Today I am Grateful For...

_____
_____
_____
_____

Date: /   /

Lord teach me to...

_____
_____
_____
_____

The Lord will fight for you; you need only to be still."
Exodus 14:14

Date: / /

Today's Verse

_____
_____
_____
_____

Date: / /

Today I am Grateful For...

_____
_____
_____
_____

Date: / /

Lord Teach me To...

_____
_____
_____
_____

"For I am the Lord your God who takes hold of your
right hand and says to you, Do not fear; I will help you."
Isaiah 41:13

Date: /   /

Today's Verse

_____
_____
_____
_____

Date: /   /

Today I am Grateful For...

_____
_____
_____
_____

Date: /   /

Lord teach me to...

_____
_____
_____
_____

"The Lord is near to all who call on Him." Psalm 145:18

Date: / /

Today's Verse

_____
_____
_____
_____

Date: / /

Today I am Grateful For...

• _____
• _____
• _____
• _____

Date: / /

Lord teach me to...

_____
_____
_____
_____

"Give thanks in all circumstances; for this is God's will
for you in Christ Jesus." Thessalonians 5:18

Date: / /

Today's Verse

_____
_____
_____
_____
_____

Date: / /

Today I am Grateful For...

_____
_____
_____
_____
_____

Date: / /

Lord teach me to...

_____
_____
_____
_____
_____

"The righteous person may have many troubles,
but the Lord delivers him from them all." Psalm 34:19

Date: /   /

Today's Verse

_____
_____
_____
_____

Date: /   /

Today I am Grateful For...

_____
_____
_____
_____

Date: /   /

Lord teach me to...

_____
_____
_____
_____

The Lord will fight for you; you need only to be still."
Exodus 14:14

Date: / /

Today's Verse

_____
_____
_____
_____

Date: / /

Today I am Grateful For...

_____
_____
_____
_____

Date: / /

Lord Teach me To...

_____
_____
_____
_____

"For I am the Lord your God who takes hold of your
right hand and says to you, Do not fear; I will help you."
Isaiah 41:13

Date: /   /

Today's Verse

_____
_____
_____
_____

Date: /   /

Today I am Grateful For...

_____
_____
_____
_____

Date: /   /

Lord teach me to...

_____
_____
_____
_____

"The Lord is near to all who call on Him." Psalm 145:18

Date: / /

Today's Verse

_____
_____
_____
_____

Date: / /

Today I am Grateful For...

- _____
- _____
- _____
- _____

Date: / /

Lord teach me to...

_____
_____
_____
_____

"Give thanks in all circumstances; for this is God's will
for you in Christ Jesus." Thessalonians 5:18

Date: / /

Today's Verse

_____
_____
_____
_____

Date: / /

Today I am Grateful For...

_____
_____
_____
_____

Date: / /

Lord teach me to...

_____
_____
_____
_____

"The righteous person may have many troubles,
but the Lord delivers him from them all." Psalm 34:19

Date: /   /

Today's Verse

_____
_____
_____
_____

Date: /   /

Today I am Grateful For...

_____
_____
_____
_____

Date: /   /

Lord teach me to...

_____
_____
_____
_____

The Lord will fight for you; you need only to be still."
Exodus 14:14

Date: / /

Today's Verse

_____
_____
_____
_____

Date: / /

Today I am Grateful For...

_____
_____
_____
_____

Date: / /

Lord Teach me To...

_____
_____
_____
_____

"For I am the Lord your God who takes hold of your
right hand and says to you, Do not fear; I will help you."
Isaiah 41:13

Date: / /

Today's Verse

_____
_____
_____
_____

Date: / /

Today I am Grateful For...

_____
_____
_____
_____

Date: / /

Lord teach me to...

_____
_____
_____
_____

"The Lord is near to all who call on Him." Psalm 145:18

Date: / /

Today's Verse

_____
_____
_____
_____

Date: / /

Today I am Grateful For...

- _____
- _____
- _____
- _____

Date: / /

Lord teach me to...

_____
_____
_____
_____

"Give thanks in all circumstances; for this is God's will for you in Christ Jesus." Thessalonians 5:18

Date: / /

Today's Verse

_____

_____

_____

_____

Date: / /

Today I am Grateful For...

_____

_____

_____

_____

Date: / /

Lord teach me to...

_____

_____

_____

_____

"The righteous person may have many troubles,
but the Lord delivers him from them all." Psalm 34:19

Date: / /

Today's Verse

_____
_____
_____
_____
_____

Date: / /

Today I am Grateful For...

_____
_____
_____
_____
_____

Date: / /

Lord teach me to...

_____
_____
_____
_____
_____

The Lord will fight for you; you need only to be still."
Exodus 14:14

Date: / /

Today's Verse

_____
_____
_____
_____

Date: / /

Today I am Grateful For...

_____
_____
_____
_____

Date: / /

Lord Teach me To...

_____
_____
_____
_____

"For I am the Lord your God who takes hold of your
right hand and says to you, Do not fear; I will help you."
Isaiah 41:13

Date: / /

Today's Verse

_____
_____
_____
_____

Date: / /

Today I am Grateful For...

_____
_____
_____
_____

Date: / /

Lord teach me to...

_____
_____
_____
_____

"The Lord is near to all who call on Him." Psalm 145:18

Date: /   /

Today's Verse

_____
_____
_____
_____

Date: /   /

Today I am Grateful For...

· _____
· _____
· _____
· _____

Date: /   /

Lord teach me to...

_____
_____
_____
_____

"Give thanks in all circumstances; for this is God's will
for you in Christ Jesus." Thessalonians 5:18

Date: /   /

Today's Verse

_____
_____
_____
_____

Date: /   /

Today I am Grateful For...

_____
_____
_____
_____

Date: /   /

Lord teach me to...

_____
_____
_____
_____

"The righteous person may have many troubles,
but the Lord delivers him from them all." Psalm 34:19

Date: / /

Today's Verse

_____
_____
_____
_____
_____

Date: / /

Today I am Grateful For...

_____
_____
_____
_____

Date: / /

Lord teach me to...

_____
_____
_____
_____

The Lord will fight for you; you need only to be still."
Exodus 14:14

Date: /   /

Today's Verse

_____
_____
_____
_____

Date: /   /

Today I am Grateful For...

_____
_____
_____
_____

Date: /   /

Lord Teach me To...

_____
_____
_____
_____

"For I am the Lord your God who takes hold of your
right hand and says to you, Do not fear; I will help you."
Isaiah 41:13

Date: /   /

Today's Verse

_____
_____
_____
_____

Date: /   /

Today I am Grateful For...

_____
_____
_____
_____

Date: /   /

Lord teach me to...

_____
_____
_____
_____

"The Lord is near to all who call on Him." Psalm 145:18

Date: / /

Today's Verse

_____

_____

_____

_____

Date: / /

Today I am Grateful For...

- _____

- _____

- _____

- _____

Date: / /

Lord teach me to...

_____

_____

_____

_____

"Give thanks in all circumstances; for this is God's will
for you in Christ Jesus." Thessalonians 5:18

Date: / /

Today's Verse

_____
_____
_____
_____

Date: / /

Today I am Grateful For...

_____
_____
_____
_____

Date: / /

Lord teach me to...

_____
_____
_____
_____

"The righteous person may have many troubles,
but the Lord delivers him from them all." Psalm 34:19

Date: /   /

Today's Verse

_____
_____
_____
_____

Date: /   /

Today I am Grateful For...

_____
_____
_____
_____

Date: /   /

Lord teach me to...

_____
_____
_____
_____

The Lord will fight for you; you need only to be still."
Exodus 14:14

Date: / /

Today's Verse

_____
_____
_____
_____

Date: / /

Today I am Grateful For...

_____
_____
_____
_____

Date: / /

Lord Teach me To...

_____
_____
_____
_____

"For I am the Lord your God who takes hold of your
right hand and says to you, Do not fear; I will help you."
Isaiah 41:13

Date: /   /

Today's Verse

_____
_____
_____
_____

Date: /   /

Today I am Grateful For...

_____
_____
_____
_____

Date: /   /

Lord teach me to...

_____
_____
_____
_____

"The Lord is near to all who call on Him." Psalm 145:18

Date: /   /

Today's Verse

_____
_____
_____
_____

Date: /   /

Today I am Grateful For...

- _____
- _____
- _____
- _____

Date: /   /

Lord teach me to...

_____
_____
_____
_____

"Give thanks in all circumstances; for this is God's will
for you in Christ Jesus." Thessalonians 5:18

Date: / /

Today's Verse

_____
_____
_____
_____

Date: / /

Today I am Grateful For...

_____
_____
_____
_____

Date: / /

Lord teach me to...

_____
_____
_____
_____

"The righteous person may have many troubles,
but the Lord delivers him from them all." Psalm 34:19

Date: /   /

Today's Verse

_____

_____

_____

_____

Date: /   /

Today I am Grateful For...

_____

_____

_____

_____

Date: /   /

Lord teach me to...

_____

_____

_____

_____

The Lord will fight for you; you need only to be still."
Exodus 14:14

Date: / /

Today's Verse

_____
_____
_____
_____

Date: / /

Today I am Grateful For...

_____
_____
_____
_____

Date: / /

Lord Teach me To...

_____
_____
_____
_____

"For I am the Lord your God who takes hold of your
right hand and says to you, Do not fear; I will help you."
Isaiah 41:13

Date: / /

Today's Verse

_____
_____
_____
_____

Date: / /

Today I am Grateful For...

_____
_____
_____
_____

Date: / /

Lord teach me to...

_____
_____
_____
_____

"The Lord is near to all who call on Him." Psalm 145:18

Date: / /

Today's Verse

_____
_____
_____
_____
_____

Date: / /

Today I am Grateful For...

- _____
- _____
- _____
- _____

Date: / /

Lord teach me to...

_____
_____
_____
_____
_____

"Give thanks in all circumstances; for this is God's will
for you in Christ Jesus." Thessalonians 5:18

Date: /   /

Today's Verse

_____
_____
_____
_____

Date: /   /

Today I am Grateful For...

_____
_____
_____
_____

Date: /   /

Lord teach me to...

_____
_____
_____
_____

"The righteous person may have many troubles,
but the Lord delivers him from them all." Psalm 34:19

Date: / /

Today's Verse

_____
_____
_____
_____

Date: / /

Today I am Grateful For...

_____
_____
_____
_____

Date: / /

Lord teach me to...

_____
_____
_____
_____

The Lord will fight for you; you need only to be still."
Exodus 14:14

Date: / /

Today's Verse

_____
_____
_____
_____

Date: / /

Today I am Grateful For...

_____
_____
_____
_____

Date: / /

Lord Teach me To...

_____
_____
_____
_____

"For I am the Lord your God who takes hold of your
right hand and says to you, Do not fear; I will help you."
Isaiah 41:13

Date: /   /

Today's Verse

_____
_____
_____
_____

Date: /   /

Today I am Grateful For...

_____
_____
_____
_____

Date: /   /

Lord teach me to...

_____
_____
_____
_____

"The Lord is near to all who call on Him." Psalm 145:18

Date: / /

Today's Verse

_____
_____
_____
_____
_____

Date: / /

Today I am Grateful For...

- _____
- _____
- _____
- _____

Date: / /

Lord teach me to...

_____
_____
_____
_____

"Give thanks in all circumstances; for this is God's will
for you in Christ Jesus." Thessalonians 5:18

Date: / /

Today's Verse

_____

_____

_____

_____

Date: / /

Today I am Grateful For...

_____

_____

_____

_____

Date: / /

Lord teach me to...

_____

_____

_____

_____

"The righteous person may have many troubles,
but the Lord delivers him from them all." Psalm 34:19

Date: /   /

Today's Verse

_____
_____
_____
_____

Date: /   /

Today I am Grateful For...

_____
_____
_____
_____

Date: /   /

Lord teach me to...

_____
_____
_____
_____

The Lord will fight for you; you need only to be still."
Exodus 14:14

Date: /   /

Today's Verse

_____
_____
_____
_____

Date: /   /

Today I am Grateful For...

_____
_____
_____
_____

Date: /   /

Lord Teach me To...

_____
_____
_____
_____

"For I am the Lord your God who takes hold of your
right hand and says to you, Do not fear; I will help you."
Isaiah 41:13

Date: /   /

Today's Verse

_____
_____
_____
_____

Date: /   /

Today I am Grateful For...

_____
_____
_____
_____

Date: /   /

Lord teach me to...

_____
_____
_____
_____

"The Lord is near to all who call on Him." Psalm 145:18

Date: / /

Today's Verse

_____

_____

_____

_____

Date: / /

Today I am Grateful For...

• _____

• _____

• _____

• _____

Date: / /

Lord teach me to...

_____

_____

_____

_____

"Give thanks in all circumstances; for this is God's will
for you in Christ Jesus." Thessalonians 5:18

Date: / /

Today's Verse

_____
_____
_____
_____

Date: / /

Today I am Grateful For...

_____
_____
_____
_____

Date: / /

Lord teach me to...

_____
_____
_____
_____

"The righteous person may have many troubles,
but the Lord delivers him from them all." Psalm 34:19

Date: / /

Today's Verse

_____
_____
_____
_____

Date: / /

Today I am Grateful For...

_____
_____
_____
_____

Date: / /

Lord teach me to...

_____
_____
_____
_____

The Lord will fight for you; you need only to be still."
Exodus 14:14

Date: / /

Today's Verse

_____

_____

_____

_____

Date: / /

Today I am Grateful For...

_____

_____

_____

_____

Date: / /

Lord Teach me To...

_____

_____

_____

_____

"For I am the Lord your God who takes hold of your
right hand and says to you, Do not fear; I will help you."
Isaiah 41:13

Date: / /

Today's Verse

_____
_____
_____
_____

Date: / /

Today I am Grateful For...

_____
_____
_____
_____

Date: / /

Lord teach me to...

_____
_____
_____
_____

"The Lord is near to all who call on Him." Psalm 145:18

Date: /   /

Today's Verse

_____
_____
_____
_____

Date: /   /

Today I am Grateful For...

• _____
• _____
• _____
• _____

Date: /   /

Lord teach me to...

_____
_____
_____
_____

"Give thanks in all circumstances; for this is God's will
for you in Christ Jesus." Thessalonians 5:18

Date: /   /

Today's Verse

_____
_____
_____
_____

Date: /   /

Today I am Grateful For...

_____
_____
_____
_____

Date: /   /

Lord teach me to...

_____
_____
_____
_____

"The righteous person may have many troubles,
but the Lord delivers him from them all." Psalm 34:19

Date: /   /

Today's Verse

_____
_____
_____
_____

Date: /   /

Today I am Grateful For...

_____
_____
_____
_____

Date: /   /

Lord teach me to...

_____
_____
_____
_____

The Lord will fight for you; you need only to be still."
Exodus 14:14

Date: / /

Today's Verse

_____
_____
_____
_____

Date: / /

Today I am Grateful For...

_____
_____
_____
_____

Date: / /

Lord Teach me To...

_____
_____
_____
_____

"For I am the Lord your God who takes hold of your
right hand and says to you, Do not fear; I will help you."
Isaiah 41:13

Date: /   /

Today's Verse

_____
_____
_____
_____

Date: /   /

Today I am Grateful For...

_____
_____
_____
_____

Date: /   /

Lord teach me to...

_____
_____
_____
_____

"The Lord is near to all who call on Him." Psalm 145:18

Date: / /

Today's Verse

_____
_____
_____
_____

Date: / /

Today I am Grateful For...

- _____
- _____
- _____
- _____

Date: / /

Lord teach me to...

_____
_____
_____
_____

"Give thanks in all circumstances; for this is God's will
for you in Christ Jesus." Thessalonians 5:18

Date: / /

Today's Verse

_____
_____
_____
_____

Date: / /

Today I am Grateful For...

_____
_____
_____
_____

Date: / /

Lord teach me to...

_____
_____
_____
_____

"The righteous person may have many troubles,
but the Lord delivers him from them all." Psalm 34:19

Date: / /

Today's Verse

_____
_____
_____
_____
_____

Date: / /

Today I am Grateful For...

_____
_____
_____
_____
_____

Date: / /

Lord teach me to...

_____
_____
_____
_____
_____

The Lord will fight for you; you need only to be still."
Exodus 14:14

Date: / /

Today's Verse

_____
_____
_____
_____

Date: / /

Today I am Grateful For...

_____
_____
_____
_____

Date: / /

Lord Teach me To...

_____
_____
_____
_____

"For I am the Lord your God who takes hold of your
right hand and says to you, Do not fear; I will help you."
Isaiah 41:13

Date: / /

Today's Verse

_____
_____
_____
_____

Date: / /

Today I am Grateful For...

_____
_____
_____
_____

Date: / /

Lord teach me to...

_____
_____
_____
_____

"The Lord is near to all who call on Him." Psalm 145:18

Date: / /

Today's Verse

_____
_____
_____
_____

Date: / /

Today I am Grateful For...

- _____
- _____
- _____
- _____

Date: / /

Lord teach me to...

_____
_____
_____
_____

"Give thanks in all circumstances; for this is God's will
for you in Christ Jesus." Thessalonians 5:18

Date: / /

Today's Verse

_____
_____
_____
_____

Date: / /

Today I am Grateful For...

_____
_____
_____
_____

Date: / /

Lord teach me to...

_____
_____
_____
_____

"The righteous person may have many troubles,
but the Lord delivers him from them all." Psalm 34:19

Today's Verse

_____
_____
_____
_____

Today I am Grateful For...

_____
_____
_____
_____

Lord teach me to...

_____
_____
_____
_____

The Lord will fight for you; you need only to be still."
Exodus 14:14

Date: / /

Today's Verse

_____
_____
_____
_____

Date: / /

Today I am Grateful For...

_____
_____
_____
_____
_____

Date: / /

Lord Teach me To...

_____
_____
_____
_____
_____

"For I am the Lord your God who takes hold of your
right hand and says to you, Do not fear; I will help you."
Isaiah 41:13

Date: / /

Today's Verse

_____
_____
_____
_____

Date: / /

Today I am Grateful For...

_____
_____
_____
_____

Date: / /

Lord teach me to...

_____
_____
_____
_____

"The Lord is near to all who call on Him." Psalm 145:18

Date: / /

Today's Verse

_____
_____
_____
_____

Date: / /

Today I am Grateful For...

- _____
- _____
- _____
- _____

Date: / /

Lord teach me to...

_____
_____
_____
_____

"Give thanks in all circumstances; for this is God's will
for you in Christ Jesus." Thessalonians 5:18

Date: /   /

Today's Verse

_____
_____
_____
_____
_____

Date: /   /

Today I am Grateful For...

_____
_____
_____
_____

Date: /   /

Lord teach me to...

_____
_____
_____
_____

"The righteous person may have many troubles,
but the Lord delivers him from them all." Psalm 34:19

Date: /   /

Today's Verse

_____
_____
_____
_____
_____

Date: /   /

Today I am Grateful For...

_____
_____
_____
_____
_____

Date: /   /

Lord teach me to...

_____
_____
_____
_____
_____

The Lord will fight for you; you need only to be still."
Exodus 14:14

Date: / /

Today's Verse

_____
_____
_____
_____

Date: / /

Today I am Grateful For...

_____
_____
_____
_____

Date: / /

Lord Teach me To...

_____
_____
_____
_____

"For I am the Lord your God who takes hold of your
right hand and says to you, Do not fear; I will help you."
Isaiah 41:13

Date: /   /

Today's Verse

_____
_____
_____
_____

Date: /   /

Today I am Grateful For...

_____
_____
_____
_____

Date: /   /

Lord teach me to...

_____
_____
_____
_____

"The Lord is near to all who call on Him." Psalm 145:18

Date: / /

Today's Verse

_____
_____
_____
_____

Date: / /

Today I am Grateful For...

• _____
• _____
• _____
• _____

Date: / /

Lord teach me to...

_____
_____
_____
_____

"Give thanks in all circumstances; for this is God's will for you in Christ Jesus." Thessalonians 5:18

Date: /   /

Today's Verse

_____
_____
_____
_____

Date: /   /

Today I am Grateful For...

_____
_____
_____
_____

Date: /   /

Lord teach me to...

_____
_____
_____
_____

"The righteous person may have many troubles,
but the Lord delivers him from them all." Psalm 34:19

Date: / /

Today's Verse

_____
_____
_____
_____

Date: / /

Today I am Grateful For...

_____
_____
_____
_____

Date: / /

Lord teach me to...

_____
_____
_____
_____

The Lord will fight for you; you need only to be still."
Exodus 14:14

Date: / /

Today's Verse

_____

_____

_____

_____

Date: / /

Today I am Grateful For...

_____

_____

_____

_____

Date: / /

Lord Teach me To...

_____

_____

_____

_____

"For I am the Lord your God who takes hold of your
right hand and says to you, Do not fear; I will help you."
Isaiah 41:13

Date: /   /

Today's Verse

_____
_____
_____
_____

Date: /   /

Today I am Grateful For...

_____
_____
_____
_____

Date: /   /

Lord teach me to...

_____
_____
_____
_____

"The Lord is near to all who call on Him." Psalm 145:18

Date: / /

Today's Verse

_____

_____

_____

_____

Date: / /

Today I am Grateful For...

- _____

- _____

- _____

- _____

Date: / /

Lord teach me to...

_____

_____

_____

_____

"Give thanks in all circumstances; for this is God's will
for you in Christ Jesus." Thessalonians 5:18

Date: /   /

Today's Verse

_____
_____
_____
_____
_____

Date: /   /

Today I am Grateful For...

_____
_____
_____
_____
_____

Date: /   /

Lord teach me to...

_____
_____
_____
_____
_____

"The righteous person may have many troubles,
but the Lord delivers him from them all." Psalm 34:19

Date: /   /

Today's Verse

_____
_____
_____
_____

Date: /   /

Today I am Grateful For...

_____
_____
_____
_____

Date: /   /

Lord teach me to...

_____
_____
_____
_____

The Lord will fight for you; you need only to be still."
Exodus 14:14

Date: / /

Today's Verse

_____
_____
_____
_____

Date: / /

Today I am Grateful For...

_____
_____
_____
_____

Date: / /

Lord Teach me To...

_____
_____
_____
_____

"For I am the Lord your God who takes hold of your
right hand and says to you, Do not fear; I will help you."
Isaiah 41:13

Date: /   /

Today's Verse

_____
_____
_____
_____

Date: /   /

Today I am Grateful For...

_____
_____
_____
_____

Date: /   /

Lord teach me to...

_____
_____
_____
_____

"The Lord is near to all who call on Him." Psalm 145:18

Date: / /

Today's Verse

_____
_____
_____
_____

Date: / /

Today I am Grateful For...

- _____
- _____
- _____
- _____

Date: / /

Lord teach me to...

_____
_____
_____
_____

"Give thanks in all circumstances; for this is God's will
for you in Christ Jesus." Thessalonians 5:18

Date: / /

Today's Verse

_____
_____
_____
_____

Date: / /

Today I am Grateful For...

_____
_____
_____
_____

Date: / /

Lord teach me to...

_____
_____
_____
_____

"The righteous person may have many troubles,
but the Lord delivers him from them all." Psalm 34:19

Date: /   /

Today's Verse

_____
_____
_____
_____

Date: /   /

Today I am Grateful For...

_____
_____
_____
_____

Date: /   /

Lord teach me to...

_____
_____
_____
_____

The Lord will fight for you; you need only to be still."
Exodus 14:14

Date: / /

Today's Verse

_____
_____
_____
_____

Date: / /

Today I am Grateful For...

_____
_____
_____
_____

Date: / /

Lord Teach me To...

_____
_____
_____
_____

"For I am the Lord your God who takes hold of your
right hand and says to you, Do not fear; I will help you."
Isaiah 41:13

Date: /   /

Today's Verse

_____
_____
_____
_____

Date: /   /

Today I am Grateful For...

_____
_____
_____
_____

Date: /   /

Lord teach me to...

_____
_____
_____
_____

"The Lord is near to all who call on Him." Psalm 145:18

Date: / /

Today's Verse

_____
_____
_____
_____

Date: / /

Today I am Grateful For...

• _____
• _____
• _____
• _____

Date: / /

Lord teach me to...

_____
_____
_____
_____

"Give thanks in all circumstances; for this is God's will
for you in Christ Jesus." Thessalonians 5:18

Date: /   /

Today's Verse

_____
_____
_____
_____

Date: /   /

Today I am Grateful For...

_____
_____
_____
_____

Date: /   /

Lord teach me to...

_____
_____
_____
_____

"The righteous person may have many troubles,
but the Lord delivers him from them all." Psalm 34:19

Date: / /

Today's Verse

_____
_____
_____
_____
_____

Date: / /

Today I am Grateful For...

_____
_____
_____
_____

Date: / /

Lord teach me to...

_____
_____
_____
_____

The Lord will fight for you; you need only to be still."
Exodus 14:14

Date: / /

Today's Verse

_____
_____
_____
_____

Date: / /

Today I am Grateful For...

_____
_____
_____
_____

Date: / /

Lord Teach me To...

_____
_____
_____
_____

"For I am the Lord your God who takes hold of your
right hand and says to you, Do not fear; I will help you."
Isaiah 41:13

Date: /   /

Today's Verse

_____
_____
_____
_____

Date: /   /

Today I am Grateful For...

_____
_____
_____
_____

Date: /   /

Lord teach me to...

_____
_____
_____
_____

"The Lord is near to all who call on Him." Psalm 145:18

Date: /   /

Today's Verse

_____
_____
_____
_____

Date: /   /

Today I am Grateful For...

• _____
• _____
• _____
• _____

Date: /   /

Lord teach me to...

_____
_____
_____
_____

"Give thanks in all circumstances; for this is God's will
for you in Christ Jesus." Thessalonians 5:18

Date: / /

Today's Verse

_____
_____
_____
_____

Date: / /

Today I am Grateful For...

_____
_____
_____
_____

Date: / /

Lord teach me to...

_____
_____
_____
_____

"The righteous person may have many troubles,
but the Lord delivers him from them all." Psalm 34:19

Date: / /

Today's Verse

_____
_____
_____
_____

Date: / /

Today I am Grateful For...

_____
_____
_____
_____

Date: / /

Lord teach me to...

_____
_____
_____
_____

The Lord will fight for you; you need only to be still."
Exodus 14:14

Date: / /

Today's Verse

_____
_____
_____
_____

Date: / /

Today I am Grateful For...

_____
_____
_____
_____
_____

Date: / /

Lord Teach me To...

_____
_____
_____
_____
_____

"For I am the Lord your God who takes hold of your
right hand and says to you, Do not fear; I will help you."
Isaiah 41:13

Made in the USA
Columbia, SC
18 May 2020